Food Chains

BY EMMA HUDDLESTON

CONTENT CONSULTANT
DANIEL ROELKE, PhD
PROFESSOR AND DEPARTMENT HEAD
DEPARTMENT OF MARINE BIOLOGY
TEXAS A&M UNIVERSITY AT GALVESTON

Kids Core
An Imprint of Abdo Publishing
abdobooks.com

abdobooks.com

Published by Abdo Publishing, a division of ABDO, PO Box 398166, Minneapolis, Minnesota 55439.

Printed in the United States of America, North Mankato, Minnesota
052021
092021

THIS BOOK CONTAINS RECYCLED MATERIALS

Cover Photo: Wirestock Images/Shutterstock Images
Interior Photos: Shutterstock Images, 4–5, 11 (leaf), 11 (caterpillar), 11 (sparrow), 11 (snake), 11 (eagle), 17, 18, 24, 29 (caterpillar), 29 (sparrow), 29 (snake), 29 (eagle); Ashish Tripurwar/Shutterstock Images, 6; Ondrej Prosicky/Shutterstock Images, 8, 25; Andrii Bezvershenko/Shutterstock Images, 11 (fungus), 29 (fungus); Luka Hercigonja/Shutterstock Images, 12; Marcin Jucha/Shutterstock Images, 14–15; Gerd Harder/Shutterstock Images, 20–21; Galyna Andrushko/Shutterstock Images, 22; Michael Potter/Shutterstock Images, 26; iStockphoto, 28 (animals); Panuwat Srijantawong/iStockphoto, 28–29 (grass); Mariia Meteleva/iStockphoto, 29 (aphid); Anuphong Panyamoon/iStockphoto, 29 (mantis)

Editor: Marie Pearson
Series Designer: Katharine Hale

Library of Congress Control Number: 2020948337

Publisher's Cataloging-in-Publication Data

Names: Huddleston, Emma, author.
Title: Food Chains / by Emma Huddleston
Description: Minneapolis, Minnesota : Abdo Publishing, 2022 | Series: Discover biology | Includes online resources and index.
Identifiers: ISBN 9781532195327 (lib. bdg.) | ISBN 9781098215637 (ebook)
Subjects: LCSH: Biology--Juvenile literature. | Food chains (Ecology)--Juvenile literature. | Food consumption--Juvenile literature. | Life sciences--Juvenile literature.
Classification: DDC 577.16--dc23

CONTENTS

Living creatures are part of the food chain.

CHAPTER 1

Energy Source

A caterpillar crawls across a twig. It pauses to eat a leaf. A sparrow flying above spots the caterpillar. The bird quickly lands and picks up the caterpillar with its beak. Then it swallows its meal.

Animals need to eat. Some eat plants, some eat other animals, and some eat both.

The next day, the sparrow rests on a branch. A snake slithers nearby. Suddenly, it lunges forward and eats the sparrow. A few months later, the snake is sunning on a rock. An eagle perched high in a tree watches. Then the eagle swoops down. It eats the snake.

With age, the eagle eventually dies. Its body lies on the ground. Flies swarm over it. Then a vulture comes to eat the remains.

What Is the Food Chain?

All animals need food to survive. Food gives them energy and **nutrients** to grow and do other activities. The food chain describes how energy and nutrients flow between living things in an ecosystem. An ecosystem is all of the living things in an area and their interactions with each other and their surroundings.

There are several levels to a food chain. The levels can be grouped into three categories.

All levels of the food chain are important for a healthy ecosystem.

They are producer, consumer, and decomposer. Producers are the first level. They take in energy from sunlight and nutrients from the environment. Plants such as trees and grass, and **algae** such as phytoplankton in the oceans, are producers. They are food for animals.

Consumers are animals that get energy and nutrients by eating plants, algae, or other animals. This category includes multiple levels of the food chain. Animals that eat plants are called herbivores. They make up the second level of the food chain, above plants. Animals that hunt and eat other animals are carnivores. They make up the third level and higher levels. Animals that eat both producers and other animals are omnivores. They are part of multiple levels. When eating berries, they are lower on a food chain. When eating other animals, they are higher on the chain.

Decomposers connect the levels of the food chain. They break down waste from animals. They help **recycle** dead animals and plants. Decomposers put nutrients back into the environment. This helps producers grow.

A food chain shows how energy and nutrients move up through the levels. It starts with a producer. A consumer eats the producer.

Scavengers and Decomposers

Two things can happen to the remains of living things. Scavengers may eat the remains and break it down into smaller pieces. Vultures, worms, termites, and dung beetles are all scavengers. Decomposers break down waste into nutrients producers can use. **Bacteria** and fungi are decomposers.

Food Chain

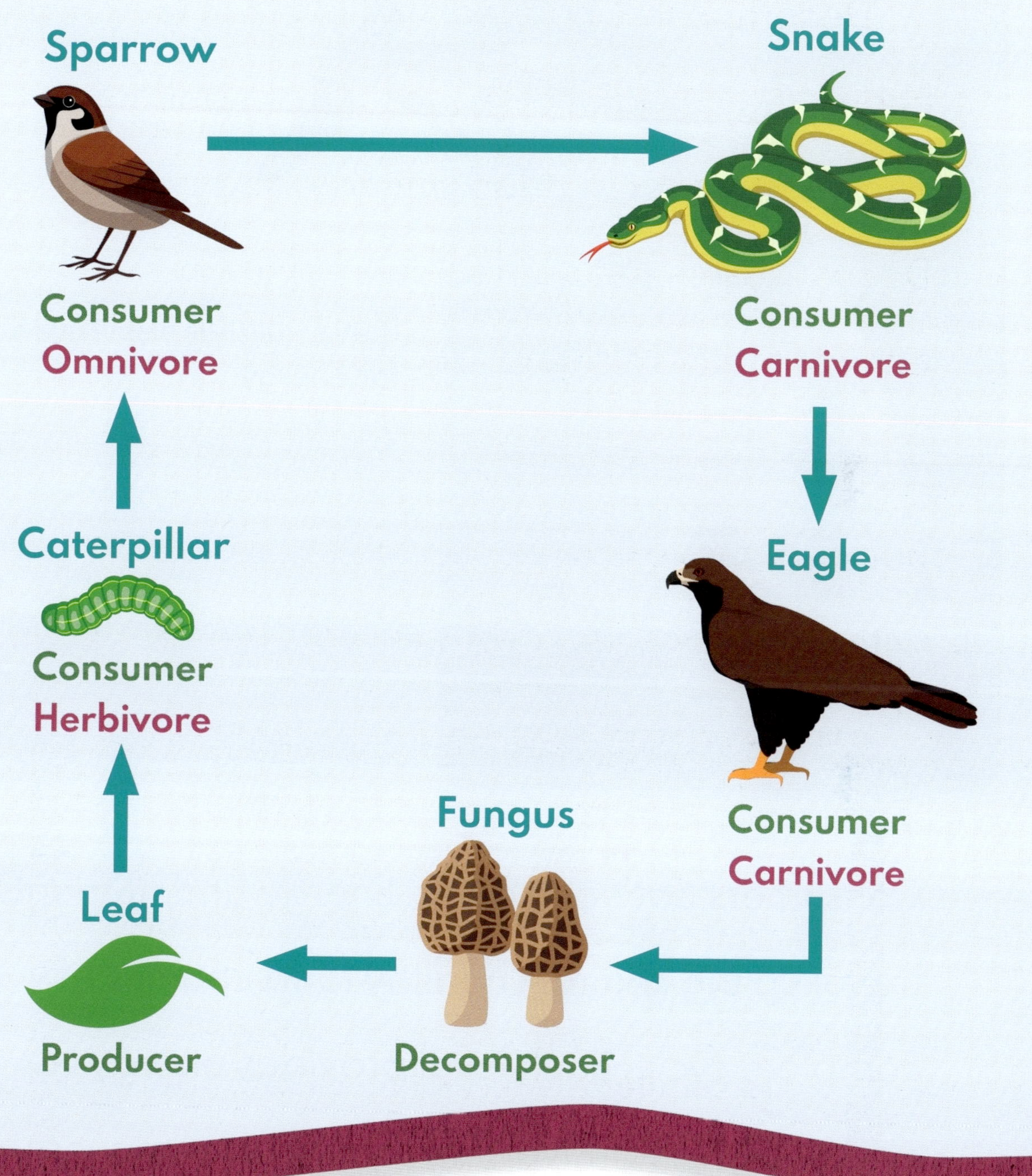

Each level of the food chain passes energy to the next. A complete chain is a cycle. Every level plays an important role.

Many animals eat insects for energy.

Consumers eat each other. Energy and nutrients travel up the chain. A healthy food chain is a complete cycle. Each level provides energy and nutrients for levels above it. Decomposers recycle the **matter**. The cycle starts again.

Primary Source

The interactions within an ecosystem include food chains. Researcher Stefani Crabtree explained that humans are also part of ecosystems:

> Ecologists typically look at ecosystems as separate from people, but to understand ecosystem health, we have to understand the people within the ecosystems.

Source: Jenna Marshall. "Study of Human Impact on Food Webs and Ecosystems." *Phys.org*, 22 Feb. 2019, phys.org. Accessed 18 May 2020.

What's the Big Idea?

Read this quote carefully. What is its main idea? Explain how the main idea is supported by details.

Many herbivores spend much of their time eating to get all of the nutrients they need.

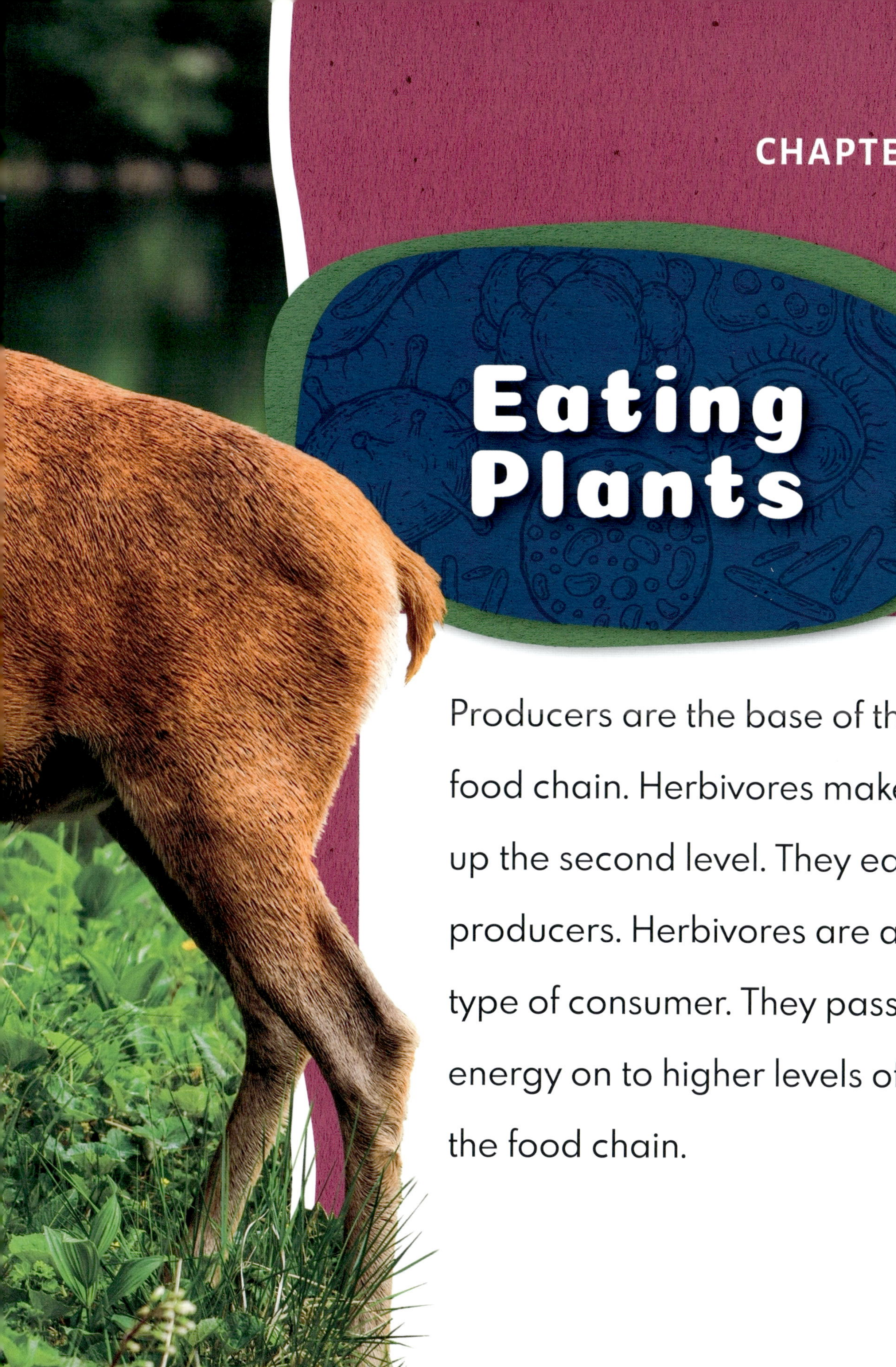

CHAPTER 2

Eating Plants

Producers are the base of the food chain. Herbivores make up the second level. They eat producers. Herbivores are a type of consumer. They pass energy on to higher levels of the food chain.

Many insects are herbivores. For example, caterpillars eat leaves. But larger animals eat plants too.

Herbivores range in size from tiny honeybees to huge elephants. Elephants eat for up to 18 hours a day. They need 290 pounds (130 kg) of food each day.

Measuring Energy

Biomass is the amount of energy in living things. Lower levels of the food chain always have more biomass. They support higher levels of the food chain. Without more biomass at the bottom, an ecosystem wouldn't have enough energy for animals at the top.

Eucalyptus leaves are poisonous to most animals. Koalas have special stomachs to eat the leaves safely.

Digesting Food

Herbivores have body parts that help them **digest** plants. Plants can have tough outer layers. So most herbivores have flat, wide teeth.

Cows have four different sections in their stomachs to digest food.

Those teeth help them grind food. Koalas eat eucalyptus leaves. They have grinding teeth and special bacteria in their guts. The bacteria break down poisonous leaf parts.

Other herbivores have special stomachs too. Sheep, camels, and cows have multiple sections in their stomachs. Food passes through each section. Eventually it softens and breaks down. The animals can then use the nutrients in the plants.

Further Evidence

Look at the website below. Does it give any new evidence about food sources to support Chapter Two?

Herbivores

abdocorelibrary.com/food-chains

Many birds, including robins, are omnivores. They will eat berries or insects.

Eating Meat

Animals that eat other animals are also consumers. They include omnivores and carnivores. Omnivores eat both meat and producers. Carnivores eat mostly meat.

Bears are omnivores that are also at the top of the food chain.

Omnivores include ants, crows, and humans. They can get energy from many sources. Omnivores eat seeds, fruit, eggs, insects, and more. They tend to make up middle levels of the food chain. But sometimes they are at the top if they eat lots of meat and don't get eaten themselves.

Carnivores are usually high on the food chain. They mainly eat meat. Some, such as cats, can eat only meat. Their bodies can't digest plant matter. They may eat herbivores, omnivores, or other carnivores.

Dealing with Change

Omnivores have a higher chance of surviving changes to the environment than other **species**. They have more food options. For example, bears eat salmon as well as roots and berries. So if there isn't enough salmon, they may be able to survive by eating plants for a time. But large carnivores may not survive a similar change.

Some predators, such as wolves, work together in groups to hunt prey.

For example, killer whales are top predators. No other animals hunt them. Killer whales eat seals and sea lions. Those animals eat fish, squids, and octopuses.

Carnivores have body parts that help them hunt. Sharp claws, teeth, or beaks help rip apart flesh. Speed helps them catch food.

One Siberian tiger can eat up to 60 pounds (27.2 kg) of food in one day.

A Balanced Ecosystem

A healthy ecosystem has fewer individual carnivores than producers, herbivores, or omnivores. If there were too many carnivores, they could take over. They would eat so much of lower levels that some species would die out. Also, larger animals tend to take up more space. For example, one Siberian tiger may hunt in a 400-square-mile (1,000-sq-km) area.

Plants and animals keep energy moving through the food web. This helps create a healthy ecosystem.

It doesn't want to compete with other tigers for food.

Food chains show how energy moves through ecosystems. Energy goes from producers to consumers to decomposers. Some chains only have three levels. Others have five or more. Often, animals eat many kinds of food. When food chains overlap, they make a food web. The web shows multiple ways energy and nutrients can travel through levels of an ecosystem.

Each food chain is unique. Every species plays a role in the energy cycle. All living things depend on the food chain to survive.

Explore Online

Visit the website below. Does it give any new information about food webs that wasn't in Chapter Three?

Food Web

abdocorelibrary.com/food-chains

Picture Biology

Bear

Wolf

Owl

Moose

Rabbit

Squirrel

Plants

A food web contains multiple food chains.

Glossary

algae
living things that resemble plants, grow in water environments, and do not have roots, stems, or leaves

bacteria
tiny living things that are made of a single cell and may be harmful or helpful

digest
to break down food into nutrients the body can use

matter
the material something is made of

nutrients
substances that living things need to grow and survive

recycle
to process so that something can be reused

species
animals that look alike and can have offspring together

Online Resources

To learn more about food chains, visit our free resource websites below.

Visit **abdocorelibrary.com** or scan this QR code for free Common Core resources for teachers and students, including vetted activities, multimedia, and booklinks, for deeper subject comprehension.

Visit **abdobooklinks.com** or scan this QR code for free additional online weblinks for further learning. These links are routinely monitored and updated to provide the most current information available.

Learn More

Duke, Shirley. *Herbivores and Carnivores Explained.* Cavendish Square, 2017.

Wilsdon, Christina. *Ultimate Predatorpedia.* National Geographic Kids, 2018.

Index

About the Author

Emma Huddleston lives in the Twin Cities in Minnesota with her husband. She enjoys reading, swing dancing, and writing books for young readers. She thinks food chains are an interesting part of nature!